RELIGIOUS LIVES

Krishna and Hinduism

Ruth Nason

HODDER
Wayland

an imprint of Hodder Children's Books

Religious Lives

The Buddha and Buddhism   Krishna and Hinduism
Guru Nanak and Sikhism   Moses and Judaism
Jesus and Christianity   Muhammad and Islam

For more information on this series and other Hodder Wayland titles, go to
www.hodderwayland.co.uk

 © White-Thomson Publishing Ltd 2006

Produced for Hodder Wayland by White-Thomson Publishing Ltd
Bridgewater Business Centre, 210 High Street, Lewes, East Sussex BN7 2NH, UK

First published in 2006 by Hodder Wayland, an imprint of Hodder Children's Books

This book is adapted from *Krishna and Hinduism* (*Great Religious Leaders* series) by Kerena Marchant, published by Hodder Wayland in 2002

British Library Cataloguing in Publication Data
Nason, Ruth
Krishna and Hinduism. - Adapted Ed. - (Religious Lives)
1. Krishna (Hindu deity) - Juvenile literature 2. Hinduism - Juvenile literature
I.Title II.Marchant, Kerena
294.5
ISBN-10: 0750247932
ISBN-13: 9780750247931
Printed in China

Hodder Children's Books
A division of Hodder Headline Limited
338 Euston Road, London NW1 3BH

Title page: Hindu women bathing in the sacred River Ganges.

Picture Acknowledgements: The publisher would like to thank the following for permission to reproduce their pictures:
AKG 7 (Jean-Louis Nou), 8 (Jean-Louis Nou), 11, 28 (Jean-Louis Nou), 43 (top) (Jean-Louis Nou); Art Directors and Trip Photo Library cover top (T Luther), 9 (H Rogers), 14 (Dinodia), 16 (T Luther), 17 (Dindodia), 18 (H Luther), 20 (Dinodia), 21 (top) (T Luther), 30 (H Rogers), 32 (Dinodia), 34 (C Wormald), 33 (Resource Foto), 36 (Dinodia), 39 (Dinodia), 40 (C Wormald), 41 (Dinodia); Chapel Studios 15 (Bob Brecher); Eye Ubiquitous title page (David Cumming), 22 (David Cumming), 23 (Bennett Dean), 27 (Chris Fairclough); Hodder Wayland Picture Library 21 (bottom); Images of India 42 (Melind A Ketkar); Impact 19 (Daniel White), 38 (Daniel White); Christine Osborne 4, 25, 31; Panos Pictures 44 (Piers Benatari); Anne and Bury Peerless 10, 12, 13; Pictorial Press; White-Thomson Publishing cover main, 19, 24, 26, 29, 33, 37, 43 (bottom) (all Chris Fairclough).

Graphics and maps by Tim Mayer.

Contents

What is Hinduism?

Hinduism is the oldest religion in the world. It began about 3000 BCE in an area around the River Indus. Hindus call it 'Hindu *Dharma*', which means the Hindu way of life.

In paintings and images, Krishna has blue skin or black skin. This shows that he was an *avatar* (earthly form) of a god called Vishnu (see page 6).

The Supreme Being

Hindus believe that all living beings are part of the Supreme Being, God. The Supreme Being is a holy spirit and has no form.

Eventually each living being will be united with the Supreme Being. Until then, each is part of a cycle of birth, death and rebirth.

Many gods = one

Long ago every village had its own god and stories about that god. Visitors heard the stories and passed them on to people in other villages. Soon villages added each other's gods to their own.

Hindus believe that all these gods are different aspects of the one Supreme Being. When they worship a god, they are worshipping one aspect of the Supreme Being: for example, god the loving mother, god the caring father, god the teacher.

Who is Krishna?

Krishna comes from a mixture of stories of gods from the south and the north of India. Some Hindus believe that Krishna is not just one aspect of the Supreme Being, but is the Supreme Being. They devote their lives to following Krishna, aiming to become free from the cycle of birth, death and rebirth.

▼ This map shows places that are important to Hindus.

The life of Krishna

Hindus believe that Krishna lived in India about 5,000 years ago. They believe he came as an *avatar* of the god Vishnu to save the world from evil. At first, Krishna worked as a cowherd in the village of Gokul. Later, he became a prince.

No evidence has been found to show if Krishna was a real prince or not.

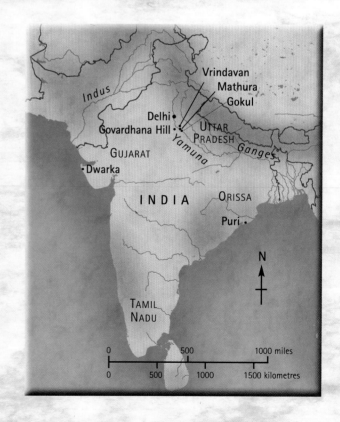

The Life of Krishna

Krishna's birth

Thousands of years ago a king called Kamsa ruled the kingdom of Mathura in north India. He was cruel and evil and everybody lived in terror of him.

Kamsa believed he would live forever. When he was told that he could only be killed by the eighth son of Devaki, his cousin's sister, he threw Devaki and her husband Vasudeva into prison. In prison the couple had children, but Kamsa killed each one.

However, when the eighth son, Krishna, was born, the prison gates magically opened and Vasudeva smuggled him out. He found a woman called Yasoda sleeping by the river with her new baby. Vasudeva swapped the babies.

When Yasoda woke up she thought that Krishna was her baby. She and her husband, Nanda, brought him up in Gokul, the cowherds' village where they lived.

An avatar of Vishnu

Hindus believe that the god Vishnu comes to save the world from evil. He comes in the form of a person or an animal. This is called an *avatar*. Hindus say that Vishnu has come to earth nine times, including the time he came as Krishna. He will come again one final time.

▲ This picture shows some scenes from Krishna's childhood. *Top left:* climbing on the shoulders of other village children to steal butter. *Bottom right:* being told off by Yasoda. *Bottom left:* allowing Yasoda to tie him up as punishment.

Krishna's childhood

Kamsa believed he had killed all Devaki's children, but he found out that Krishna was alive. He sent a demon in disguise to poison him, but the baby Krishna knew who she was and sucked her life from her.

Krishna was a naughty child and played tricks on the villagers. For example, he untied the cows and watched everybody trying to catch them. Yasoda tried to punish him. She did not know that he was also a powerful god. Krishna always took her punishment in the end because he loved her.

The cowherds and the milkmaids

When he grew up, Krishna worked as a cowherd in his village. The other cowherds and the milkmaids did not know he was the god Vishnu in human form. They loved him as a normal human friend.

Krishna was good-looking with long dark hair and brown eyes. He played the flute and was good fun. All the young milkmaids hoped he would fall in love with them.

Krishna and Radha

Krishna fell in love with Radha. He played the flute to her while she milked the cows. He liked her sense of fun and decided to play a trick on her.

◀ Krishna with the milkmaids. Paintings from south India show Krishna with black skin.

▼ Krishna and Radha.

He hid behind some bushes with his friends. When Radha and her friends passed by, the young men jumped out and threw paint over them. Radha was quick to grab some paint and throw it all over Krishna. Soon everybody was covered in paint.

That night Krishna played his flute. Radha went to him and they danced together. She loved him so much that she wanted them to get married. But soon, events were to end Krishna's happy life among the cowherds.

Dancing for Krishna

Hindus worship Krishna through dance. Indian dance is done barefoot and facial expressions, hand movements and footwork all have particular meanings. The *Rasa* dance tells the story of Krishna dancing in the woods with the milkmaids. A style of dance called *Odissi* tells the story of Krishna and Radha.

Helping the cowherds

One day the cowherds were concentrating on a game and suddenly realized that the cows had strayed away. They could not find them and began to panic.

Krishna called out the cows' names and they mooed back. Only Krishna could hear them. They sounded in distress. Krishna led the cowherds to the cows, who were surrounded by a forest fire.

Krishna said to the cowherds: 'Don't be afraid. Close your eyes, and don't open them until I ask you.' Then he sucked all the fire towards him and swallowed it.

'Now open your eyes, my friends.' The boys opened their eyes and saw that they were back where they had been playing and all the cows were with them.

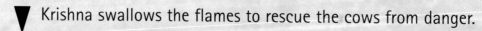

▼ Krishna swallows the flames to rescue the cows from danger.

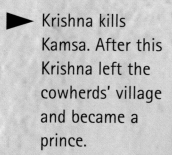 Krishna kills Kamsa. After this Krishna left the cowherds' village and became a prince.

Krishna kills King Kamsa

Kamsa called Krishna to fight a mighty wrestler called Chanura. Many of the cowherds went to watch the fight.

Chanura tried to stab Krishna with a poisoned dagger, but Krishna ducked and Chanura accidentally killed himself. Then Krishna grabbed Kamsa by the hair and swung him round. With a stamp of his foot, Krishna opened up the earth and flung Kamsa down into a fiery pit.

People were full of joy that Kamsa was dead. Krishna set Devaki and Vasudeva free and they said he was their son.

What happened to Radha?

There are many stories, songs and dances about this. One song says that when Krishna became a prince, she knew she could never marry him. She drowned herself in the River Ganges. However, her love for Krishna was so great that she could not die and the gods took her into the heavens and made her one of them.

Krishna the warrior and prince

After killing Kamsa, Krishna brought the true king, Ugrasena, back to rule Mathura. Now Krishna was going to become a warrior and prince. He sadly left his friends and foster parents in the cowherds' village.

Kamsa's queen wanted revenge for his death and sent her brother, King Jarasandha, to Mathura with his army. Krishna drove him away, but every year Jarasandha and his army returned. After 18 years, Krishna moved the kingdom to the western coast of India. He built a beautiful city there, named Dwarka.

A princess called Rukmini fell in love with Krishna, but a different marriage had been arranged for her. Krishna fetched her away in his chariot to become his queen.

◀ Krishna throws a discus in a battle. This weapon is associated with the god Vishnu.

Rukmini

Rukmini is said to be an *avatar* of the goddess Lakshmi, the wife of Vishnu. Temples to Rukmini, and images of her, usually stand close to Krishna temples and images.

▶ Rukmini and Krishna on the way to their wedding.

The end of Krishna's life on earth

Krishna ruled Dwarka for 100 years and was a greatly respected prince. Then one day his people drank too much wine and killed each other in a drunken brawl. Only Krishna survived and sat under a tree meditating. A hunter saw his foot, mistook him for a deer, and fired an arrow which pierced his heel. This was the end of Krishna's life on earth.

As an *avatar*, Krishna had destroyed evil and brought back the right way of life. But nothing of Krishna remained on earth. When he died his body became like a bright light and disappeared. All his family were dead and soon after he died, the sea swallowed up his city of Dwarka.

The Sacred Texts

Some religions have just one holy book, but Hinduism has many sacred texts. The earliest were composed about 3,000 years ago. For a long time they were remembered and passed on by word of mouth. Later they were written down in the ancient Indian language called Sanskrit.

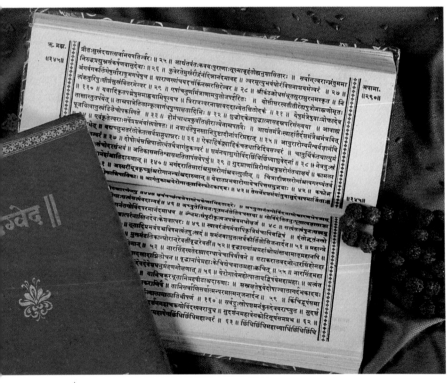

Krishna in the sacred texts

Stories about Krishna are not part of the earliest Hindu scriptures. Krishna is first mentioned in a poem called the *Mahabharata*, written between 600 BCE and 200 CE. In this poem Krishna is the respected prince of Dwarka. There is no reference to him as a cowherd.

▲ The *Rig Veda* is one of the earliest Hindu sacred texts. It contains hymns praising gods and goddesses.

The stories of Krishna the cowherd and the killing of King Kamsa come from the *Bhagavatam*, a collection of stories about the *avatars* of Vishnu. Other texts called the *Puranas*, written in the period 300-1200 CE, contain more stories about Krishna.

'AUM'

The symbol on the wall of the Hindu temple in this photograph is called 'AUM'. Hindus chant the sound 'AUM' at the beginning and end of prayers to Krishna. The symbol and the sound are sacred. They are said to represent the Supreme Being.

The past, present and the future and that which is outside time. Everything is AUM.
(Mandukya Upanishad)

▲ A priest at a Hindu temple. The food on the tray beside him has been offered to the god.

Songs, poems and dances

The story of Krishna's love for Radha is found in the many songs, poems and dances that have been created about his life and teachings. More have been written about Krishna than any other Hindu god. The songs, poems and dances are often performed in Hindu temples (also called *mandirs*).

The Mahabharata

The *Mahabharata* ('the history of Great India') is an
'epic poem' – one that tells the story of heroic deeds
in a grand way.

Its 100,000 verses tell of a feud, which began when King
Dhritarastra handed his throne to his brother, Pandu.
Pandu's sons (called the Pandavas) and the sons of
Dhritarastra (the Kauravas) argued about who should
rule when Pandu died. Krishna, the prince of Dwarka,
was a cousin of both groups. He was asked to help
settle the feud.

To start with, the Pandavas and Kauravas
took half the kingdom each, but this did
not work. They played a game of dice
to decide who would get the whole
kingdom. The Kauravas cheated
and won the game. The Pandavas
were sent into exile.

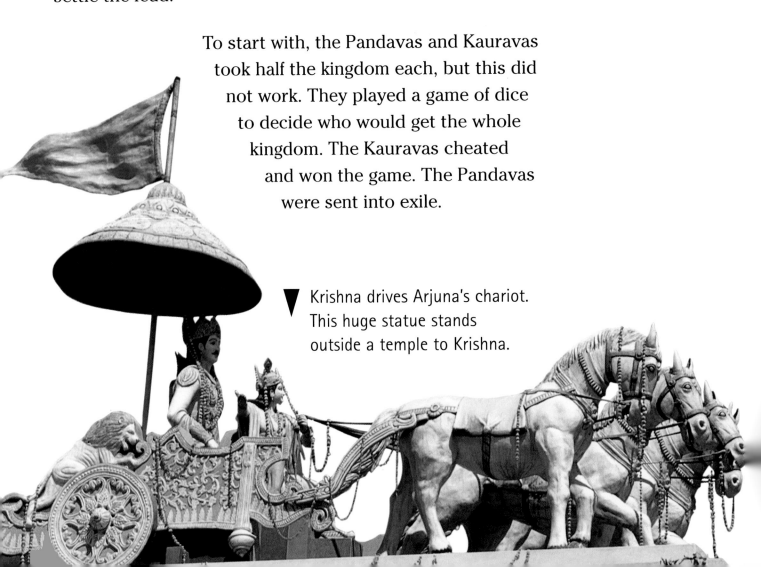

▼ Krishna drives Arjuna's chariot.
This huge statue stands
outside a temple to Krishna.

Performing the Mahabharata

In the past, actors and dancers travelled across India, performing stories from the poem. Performances started at about 7pm and went on until 7am.

In modern India, films and television dramas are made of the story. The films last for many hours. Audiences gather in huge outdoor cinemas and watch the film through the night.

▲ A scene from the *Mahabharata* is filmed for television.

The battle of Kurukshetra

After thirteen years the two sides were ready for battle and both asked Krishna to fight with them. Krishna said they could choose between having him (but he would not fight) and having his army. The Pandavas chose Krishna and the Kauravas chose his army.

During the battle Krishna drove a chariot for one of the Pandavas, called Arjuna, and advised him on the battlefield. The Pandavas won the battle and the eldest, Prince Yudhisthira, was crowned emperor of India.

The Bhagavad Gita

Many readers think that the most important part of the *Mahabharata* is a section called the *Bhagavad Gita*. Some scholars believe this was written after the rest of the poem. It is the only place where Krishna's teachings are found.

▲ Krishna and Arjuna on the battlefield.

For Hindus, Krishna is a god of love, showing them a way – through loving him – to become united with the Supreme Being (see page 4).

The *Bhagavad Gita* is a series of conversations between Arjuna and Krishna, when Krishna was driving Arjuna's chariot in the battle of Kurukshetra (see page 17).

The conversations are about the meaning of life and the way to salvation. Krishna reveals himself as God, the Supreme Being.

Many Hindus believe that the *Bhagavad Gita* is the most important sacred text. Hindu leaders and thinkers use it to guide their thoughts and actions.

An Indian holy man studies the *Bhagavad Gita*.

Although Hindus have many sacred texts, the *Bhagavad Gita* is considered the holy book of India. It is used, for example, when taking an oath in the law courts.

Mahatma Gandhi

Mahatma Gandhi (1869-1948) led a peaceful protest movement for India to become independent from British rule. India became independent in 1947. Gandhi read the *Bhagavad Gita* every day. He believed that all his actions were for God.

Krishna's Teachings

In the *Bhagavad Gita* Arjuna realizes that Krishna is the Supreme Being, God. He does not just represent one aspect of the Supreme Being. Therefore, Krishna's teachings in the *Bhagavad Gita* can be seen as teachings from God.

The Supreme Being is in humans

Krishna's life on earth is said to prove that the Supreme Being is present in all human beings. Krishna was not only a mighty warrior and a wise prince but also a cowherd, a handsome young lover and a naughty child. And so, if the Supreme Being is in all people, then it is possible for all people to be united with the Supreme Being.

Everyone is reborn

In the *Bhagavad Gita* Arjuna is worried about killing his cousins in the battle of Kurukshetra. Krishna tells him that every spirit is part of the Supreme Being and so is eternal and can never die. If Arjuna kills someone, their spirit

People believe that Krishna was the Supreme Being, even when he was a naughty child.

Arjuna recognizes Krishna as the Supreme Being and Krishna blesses him.

will either be reborn in another body, or will be united with the Supreme Being.

Hindus are cremated when they die. The ashes are immersed in a sacred river.

The cycle of rebirth

Hindus believe that, after they die, their spirit is reborn in the body of a human or other creature. Their actions in the present affect how they will be reborn.

As a man throws away used and worn-out clothes, so does the spirit leave worn-out bodies after death to enter new ones.

(*Bhagavad Gita*, 2 [22])

▲ A Hindu holy man, or *sadhu*, in India.

Becoming united with Krishna

The main aim for Hindus is to become free from the cycle of rebirth, to be united with the Supreme Being. In the *Bhagavad Gita*, Krishna tells Arjuna how people can try to achieve this. One way is through yoga.

In the West, we may think of yoga as exercises to help us stretch and relax. For Hindus, yoga means much more, including reading the scriptures, practising yoga exercise, chanting mantras and prayer. Some Hindu priests and holy men, called *sadhus*, devote their whole life to practising yoga in this way, to try to unite with the Supreme Being. The word 'yoga' means 'unite'.

Krishna's teaching was very important because he explained a way by which ordinary people can seek to be united with the Supreme Being. *Karma-yoga* means doing every action in your everyday life for Krishna (see pages 24-25) and *bhakti-yoga* means devotion to Krishna – putting Krishna at the centre of your life (see pages 16-27).

▼ Hindus who spend the end of their lives as hermits, concentrating on God, are called *sanyassins*.

Sanyassins

Some Hindus live ordinary lives until they are elderly. Then they give up everything – wife, home and family – and live as hermits. The purpose is to concentrate on seeking to be united with the Supreme Being.

The law of karma

A Hindu belief is that all actions have their effects. A good action is said to make good *karma* and good things will follow. A bad action makes bad *karma* and bad things will result.

Because of this, Hindus believe that when they die, the body in which they are reborn will depend on whether their actions have been good or bad.

In the *Bhagavad Gita* Arjuna worries that if he kills people, he will make bad *karma*. Krishna says that Arjuna is a warrior. A warrior's duty is to fight, in order to remove evil, and doing one's duty does not create bad *karma*.

▲ Many people in India live in great poverty. The idea of *karma* is that good actions will result in a better life.

Karma-yoga: every action for Krishna

Krishna says that worrying too much about doing good things and avoiding bad ones can tie people to the world. A better way to become free from the

Varnas

An ancient Hindu belief is that God created four groups of people, called *Varnas*:

Brahmin: e.g. priests
Kshatriya: e.g. rulers and warriors
Vaishya: e.g. traders
Shudra: e.g. craftsmen

Each group had particular duties so that society worked well.

Later, other ideas were introduced in India, dividing society into many small groups called castes. Some castes were thought to be better than others and people from different castes were not allowed to mix.

The ideas about castes had nothing to do with the Hindu religion.

cycle of rebirth is always to act out of love for Krishna. People's actions then will bring them closer to the Supreme Being.

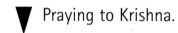
Praying to Krishna.

Bhakti-yoga: devotion to Krishna

Krishna taught that the best way to be united with him, the Supreme Being, was to love him. In the *Bhagavad Gita*, Krishna says that he will accept anything that is offered to him in love, whoever offers it. It could be offered by a priest, a king or the lowliest of people.

There is a story that one follower of Krishna was so overcome by love that he accidentally offered Krishna banana skins instead of the bananas. Krishna ate the skins gladly because they were given in love.

▼ Musicians at a Krishna temple in north India. They offer their music to Krishna as a sign of devotion.

► This shrine to Krishna in a family home in the UK has been decorated with lights for the festival of Diwali (see page 42).

Followers of Krishna show their love for him in many ways. In their homes they have a shrine to Krishna, and Krishna is at the centre of all family life.

People have created beautiful art, dance and music about Krishna. Religious thinkers have spent years writing books about him.

The teachings of Krishna have also inspired political leaders. Mahatma Gandhi (see page 19) was guided by the *Bhagavad Gita.* Other leaders have been influenced by Gandhi's example in working for a better world for all.

Equality in devotion

Krishna's teaching in the *Bhagavad Gita* was new and radical. He showed how all people, however humble, could be united with the Supreme Being. He would accept an offering from anybody, as long as it was offered in love.

Krishna and Food

Krishna was brought up as a cowherd and cows were very dear to him. He is sometimes called Gopala, which means 'Lord of the Cows'.

Pictures of Krishna

Many pictures show Krishna caring for cows, who look lovingly back at him. Also, in many pictures, the cows with Krishna have garlands around their necks and peacock feathers on their heads. These decorations are signs of respect.

▼ These modern cows are covered in gold decorations for a festival.

Cows

The Hindu scriptures say that to kill and eat a cow or her calf is a great sin:

All who eat the flesh or permit the slaughter of cows will rot in hell for as many years as there are hairs on the cow's body.
(Puranas)

In parts of India where people do not have cars or farm machinery, bulls are still used for pulling carts and other heavy work.

Cows are sacred

For Hindus, the cow is sacred because she is the symbol of Mother Earth. The cow provides milk and other dairy foods, which help keep humans healthy.

Because of their beliefs about cows, Hindus forbid the eating of beef. In fact, many Hindus are vegetarians: i.e. they do not eat any kind of meat.

In India, cows are allowed to roam free and live out their natural life. It used to be quite common to find a cow lying in a city street causing a traffic jam. Today there are sanctuaries to keep cows safely away from busy streets.

Food for Krishna

When Hindus worship Krishna, they offer him food. They try to give food that they know Krishna likes.

Stories about his childhood show that he loved dairy foods. He loved butter so much that he would steal it (see page 7).

In the *Bhagavad Gita*, Krishna lists dairy products, grains, fruits and vegetables as healthy foods to eat. He does not eat meat because all life forms are part of the Supreme Being and deserve equal respect.

Prashad

When worshippers offer food to Krishna and to other Hindu gods, the food becomes *prashad*. The worshippers believe that the god blesses the food. Afterwards it is shared among the worshippers.

▼ In the cowherds' village where he grew up, Krishna was called 'the butter thief'. The villagers tried to hide butter from him, but he always found it.

Eating prashad

A saying among followers of Krishna is that if you eat ordinary food, you develop desires for material things. If you eat *prashad*, you increase your love of God with every mouthful.

◀ Food is offered to the Hindu gods not just at festivals, as here, but as part of all worship.

Followers of Krishna offer him food when they worship him at a temple. Also at home, before they eat together, they offer their food to Krishna. They only eat food that is *prashad*.

The Sacred Places

Hindu pilgrims visit places around India that are associated with the stories of the different gods. In some of these places there are famous temples or shrines. There are also seven sacred rivers in India.

▼ Pilgrims on their way to the *Maha-Kumba* festival.

Reasons for going on pilgrimage

Often Hindus go to a sacred river to bathe and purify themselves. When a loved one has died and been cremated, Hindus go to scatter or immerse the ashes in the river.

Sacred rivers

Hindus believe that the Ganges is the most sacred river in India. A story says it was created by the god Vishnu. He pierced the earth with his toenail and the pure waters gushed out.

The River Yamuna is associated with Krishna and Radha. A festival called *Maha-Kumba* takes place every 12 years where the Ganges and Yamuna rivers merge.

▲ This is the River Yamuna at Vrindavan (see page 34).

Some people go on pilgrimage to make amends for a wrongdoing. Some visit shrines where they believe they can be healed from an illness or disability. Huge crowds of pilgrims gather in some places to celebrate certain festivals.

Pilgrims for Krishna

Followers of Krishna go to places where he is said to have lived. They also visit temples dedicated to Krishna, in India and in other countries including Britain, Canada and the USA. Making a pilgrimage to one of these places is an act of devotion to Krishna.

Places associated with Krishna

Followers of Krishna visit Mathura, where he was born; Gokul, where he was brought up; Vrindavan, where he played with the milkmaids; and Dwarka. They also go to Puri, which has a famous Krishna temple. In Puri, Krishna is known as 'Lord Jagannath' and there is a festival to honour him every year.

Vrindavan

Vrindavan is a peaceful rural area with many temples to Krishna and Radha. Festivals are held at the temples to remember events in Krishna's life as a cowherd.

Near Vrindavan is a hill called Govardhana Hill. It is said that Krishna lifted this hill and held

▼ A temple in Vrindavan. Hindu temples are built high so that pilgrims can see them from a distance.

it over the villagers to shelter them from the rain sent by the god Indra (see page 42).

Dwarka

The present-day city of Dwarka is small. It is not the city called Dwarka that Krishna ruled (see pages 12 and 13).

In Dwarka, Krishna is known as Lord Dwarkadeesh and there is a large temple to him. Outside the city there is a temple to Rukmini, Krishna's queen. Rukmini is worshipped there not only as Krishna's wife but also as an *avatar* of Lakshmi (see page 13).

Non-Hindu visitors

Non-Hindus who want to visit the temple at Dwarka must fill in a form to prove that they have some commitment to Hinduism and Krishna. They must also present an offering or a prayer to Krishna as Lord Dwarkadeesh.

▲ Pilgrims outside the temple to Krishna in Dwarka.

Festivals

The year is full of festivals to celebrate the birthdays and other special times in the lives of the gods. Different gods are important in different places, and so festivals vary around India.

Preparing for a festival

At home, before a festival, the family prepares a feast for the god, including his or her favourite food and lots of sweets. In temples, priests make similar preparations.

▼ Pilgrims arrive in Uttar Pradesh for the *Maha-Kumba* festival.

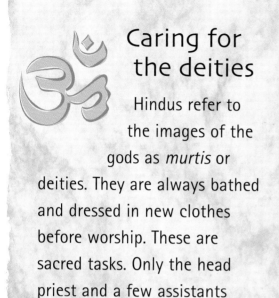

Caring for the deities

Hindus refer to the images of the gods as *murtis* or deities. They are always bathed and dressed in new clothes before worship. These are sacred tasks. Only the head priest and a few assistants may touch the deities.

▲ This young priest is lighting a lamp for the festival of Diwali.

Priests and other people also get ready for the festival by fasting and reading the sacred texts.

Celebrating a festival

A festival can last for several days. During this time people go to worship in the temple, and dancers and actors perform the festival stories.

Sometimes the images of the gods are taken out of the temple and driven through the town on carts. For some festivals, special giant images of the god are made and these are paraded around the town. At the end of the festival the giant images are lowered into a sacred river or lake.

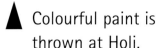
Colourful paint is thrown at Holi.

Holi (February/March)

Holi is a spring festival, celebrated all over India. It is a tradition to throw coloured powder or coloured water over each other – as Krishna and Radha did (see page 9). There may also be fireworks and bonfires.

Jagannath Festival (June/July)

This festival is held at the temple in Puri. Many pilgrims travel there for the festival, which celebrates Krishna as Lord Jagannath, the Lord of the Universe.

Giant images of Krishna and his brother and sister are placed on decorated chariots. Then the heavy chariots are

Festival dates

The dates of festivals are fixed on the Hindu calendar, where each month begins when a new moon appears. The difference between the Hindu calendar and the Western calendar means that the dates of festivals vary from year to year on the Western calendar.

pulled from the temple to the other end of the town. The Raja (prince) of Puri sweeps the ground in front of the chariots, to show that all people are equal in Krishna's eyes.

The chariots stay at the other end of the town for a week. Each day the images are dressed in new clothes, and freshly cooked food is offered to them and shared with the pilgrims as *prashad*. Then the images are taken back to the temple.

Food for pilgrims

The priests at the temple at Puri cook chick-pea and dried-fruit balls the size of Lord Jagannath's fist, to share out to the pilgrims for their journey home.

▼ The three giant chariots at Puri are about 13 metres high and have 18 wheels.

The Swing Festival (July/August)

This festival celebrates the love of Krishna and Radha (see pages 8-9). In temples in Vrindavan, the images of Krishna and Radha are put on to gold and silver swings. In Orissa, temple dances tell the love story.

Janmashtami (August/September)

This is the festival for Krishna's birth (see page 6). It is celebrated all over India.

Followers of Krishna pray and fast to prepare for the festival. They remember that Krishna came to earth to save the world from evil. The fast ends at midnight on the night when the new moon appears. This is the time of Krishna's birth.

At midnight people go to worship at Krishna temples. In many, the image of Krishna (the deity) is washed in holy water from a sacred river and purified with milk and honey. The deity is then dressed in special clothes and placed in a cradle.

▲ Krishna and Radha on a swing, in a painting at a temple in Vrindavan.

Some pilgrims travel to Mathura, Krishna's birthplace. They also visit Gokul, where Krishna's foster parents celebrated his birth 5,000 years ago.

Radhastami (August/September)

This festival celebrates the birth of Radha and falls 15 days after Krishna's birthday. Worshippers go to the temple with offerings for Radha.

Celebrating Janmashtami

Hindus believe that it is important to celebrate Krishna's birthday. One of the sacred texts says:

If one neglects to celebrate the birthday of Lord Krishna ... one will be reborn as a serpent in a deep forest.
(Bhavishya Purana)

At Krishna's birthday festival people make human pyramids, remembering how Krishna climbed up to find butter when he was a child (see page 7).

Diwali (October/November)

Diwali is the most popular Hindu festival. It is celebrated in late autumn, as the evenings become darker. Lights are placed at windows and doors.

There are different stories, about different gods, behind the Diwali celebrations. The stories are all about the triumph of good over evil. Followers of Krishna remember how Krishna killed a cruel demon called Narakasura.

Govardhana Hill Puja (October/November)

The story behind this festival is that, once, Krishna thought that the god Indra had become too proud. He ordered the cowherds not to make offerings to Indra but to Govardhana Hill instead. Indra sent torrential rain to punish the villagers. Krishna lifted

▲ Shops are decorated with lights for Diwali and people buy cards, sweets and presents for the festival.

▶ Krishna lifts the hill, to show that he was more powerful than Indra.

up Govardhana Hill and held it over the people to shelter them.

During the festival people make hills from cow dung or sacred food and circle round them in worship. Food is placed on Govardhana Hill (see page 34). This shows caring for the mountain and for the environment.

Gita Jayanti (December)

This is known as the birthday of the *Bhagavad Gita* (see pages 18-19). The festival is celebrated in Kurukshetra, to mark the day when Krishna gave his teachings to Arjuna on the battlefield.

▶ Carrying cow dung home as fuel.

Cow dung

Hindus in India use cow dung as fuel and for cleaning their homes and purifying temples for worship. Cow dung might smell but it has antiseptic qualities. It can be made into soap to cure skin diseases.

Hinduism Today

Krishna appeals to people from all backgrounds, from richest to poorest. He is the God who loves everybody and attracts love in return. Krishna's influence can be seen in many places.

Hindu material for sale at a market stall includes a picture of Krishna as a child.

In India, market stallholders sell cards and pictures of Krishna. Some of the best-selling books are stories of the *Mahabharata* (see pages 16-17). Outdoor cinemas are full of people watching films based on the *Mahabharata*.

Krishna and politics

In the twentieth century, Krishna's teachings about equality became part of Indian politics. Mahatma Gandhi (see page 19) was influenced by the *Bhagavad Gita*. He campaigned for equality for all the people of India. The poorest had been classed as 'Untouchables' and strict rules banned them from many places. Gandhi called these people 'the children of God'. As a result of the campaign he started, it was made illegal to treat anyone as 'Untouchable'.

Krishna in the Western world

Hinduism is the third largest religion with about 850,000,000 members. 95 per cent live in India. Hindus have moved to other countries, including the USA, Britain and Canada, but do not try to change other people to their religion.

However, people in the West have been attracted to Krishna. In the 1960s many people called for peace and love in society. A Hindu guru, Srila Bhaktivedanta Prabhupada, travelled to the West to teach about Krishna. Later the International Society for Krishna Consciousness (ISKCON) was formed. Today groups of followers chanting 'Hare Krishna' are a familiar sight in Western city streets.

A god of love, for everyone

Krishna brings a message of equality and love. All people are part of the Supreme Being, God. Every spirit is eternal and can be united with God.

▲ Members of The Beatles with a Hindu guru called the Maharishi, in 1968.

Krishna in the 'Top Ten'

George Harrison, one of The Beatles, wrote a song to Krishna called 'My Sweet Lord'. It reached the Top Ten in the pop charts. He also donated a stately home to ISKCON: Bhaktivedanta Manor in the UK.

Glossary

avatar   a Hindu word that means 'to come down'. Hindus believe that Vishnu and some other gods come down to earth in different forms, called *avatars*.

BCE   before the Common Era, an alternative for BC (Before Christ). The system of counting years BC and AD (Anno Domini – 'in the year of our Lord') is used worldwide. It is based on Christian belief in Jesus. Out of respect for people who follow religions other than Christianity, BC and AD are replaced with BCE and CE (Common Era).

bless   to wish great happiness on someone, from God; or to make something holy.

cremated   burned to ashes.

deity   the word that many Hindus use for the images of the gods in temples and shrines. Deity means a god or goddess.

demon   an evil spirit or devil.

devotion   giving all one's love and attention.

dharma   a Hindu word for duty, or right way of living, or religion.

fast   to go without food for a certain period, as a kind of self-sacrifice. People often fast to help them focus their mind on religious thoughts.

garland   a necklace of flowers, given to show love and respect.

guru   a religious teacher or guide.

holy   concerned with God or religion, sacred.

image   in Hindu temples and shrines, a picture or a statue of a god. The images are treated with great care and respect. Hindus refer to them as 'deities' or '*murtis*'.

mandir   a Hindu temple.

mantra   a sound, word or prayer, often repeated as part of worship or meditation.

meditate   to spend time quietly thinking and reflecting over spiritual things.

offerings   gifts made to a god as part of worship.

pilgrims   people who travel to a holy place for religious reasons.

prashad   food that has been offered to a Hindu deity or deities and is shared by worshippers.

purify   to make pure and free from anything bad or evil.

sacred   connected to God, holy.

sadhu   a Hindu holy man who has devoted his life to praying and meditating. People give the *sadhus* the food and money they need to survive.

salvation   being saved or rescued from sin and its results.

shrine   a holy place associated with a god.

temple   a building where Hindu people go to worship. Another name used for a Hindu temple is *mandir*.

worship   to respect and adore something, and also to show respect and adoration.

Further Information

Books

Festivals. Diwali by Kerena Marchant (Hodder Wayland, 1999)

Hindu Festivals Through the Year by Anita Ganeri (Franklin Watts, 2003)

My Hindu Community by Kate Taylor (Franklin Watts, 2005)

Religions of the World. The Hindu World by Patricia Bahree (Hodder Wayland, 2001)

Storyteller: Hindu Stories by Anita Ganeri (Evans Publishing Group, 2000)

The Facts About Hinduism by Alison Cooper (Hodder Children's, 2004)

World of Festivals: Divali by Dilip Kadodwala (Evans Publishing Group, 2004)

World of Festivals: Holi by Dilip Kadodwala (Evans Publishing Group, 2004)

Resources for teachers

http://www.reonline.org.uk
A 'family of websites' including some for teachers and some for pupils. Serves as a gateway to over 300 RE resources drawn from all over the web.

http://re-xs.ucsm.ac.uk
RE Exchange Service (linked to National Grid for Learning) with a 'Teachers' Cupboard' resource page.

http://www.theredirectory.org.uk

http://www.iskcon.org

http://www.hindunet.org

BBC Education produces schools media resources on different faiths. See: http://www.bbc.co.uk/schools

Channel 4 produces schools media resources on different faiths, including *Animated World Faiths*. Download catalogue from: http://www.channel4.com/learning

The Institute for Indian Art and Culture
The Bhavan Centre, 4a Castletown Road, West Kensington, London W14 9HQ
Tel: 0207 381 3086   http://www.bhavan.net

Hindu Sahitya Kendra (Hindu Literature Shop)
46-48 Loughborough Road, Leicester LE4 5LD
Tel: 0116 261 1303   Fax: 0116 261 1931

Index